Wine Cork Crafting

Craft Design AND Fun
The Wine Cork Craft Guide

By Daniel Lucas
Daniel@corkcrafting.com

What are corks?	i
Easy Refrigerator Magnets	7
Cool Picture Frame	10
Nifty Table Trivet	19
Distinctive Wine Rack	24
Effective Drink Coasters	36
Single Wine Bottle Holder	40
Aquarium Sailboat	53
Detailed Model Airplane	56
Super Simple Model Car	62
Floating Castaway Sailboat	66
Fancy European Car Model	70
Civil War Cannon	76
Creative Birdhouse	82
Cool Universal Golf Putter	113
Crafty Napkin Holder	120
Useful Cell Phone or Tablet Stand	128
Elegant Business Card Holder	136
Additional Cork Crafting Ideas	140

Where do corks come from? Almost every winery in the world uses corks but where are they originated from?

Corks come from a tree commonly called the Cork Oak. Portugal is considered the cork capital of the world and most of the corks come from there. Corks come in all shapes, sizes, and varieties. The corks used on these projects measure about 1 ¾ inches in height standing up. If yours are not this size, no worries as long as they are corks, they will work for all the projects in this book. There are real corks and synthetic corks. Synthetic corks have a more solid and rubber look to them. Synthetic corks are more similar in size and shape than real corks. There are also champagne corks which are usually real corks but are designed a little different. I mainly used plain, real corks but there were some projects I tried with synthetic. Most of the corks I used were regular corks meaning they didn't have any designs or writings on them. They were not anything fancy, just plain corks. You can, however, use any corks for all the projects in this book. Using corks with designs and writings on them adds more uniqueness to the projects you are creating. The only concern with using any corks that have designs etched in the cork is getting the glue to stick. Synthetic corks and plain real corks will not have any problem.

If you need more corks than what you already have, here are a few good resources you can try. Check with your local winery about what they do with their used corks. If you have a local wine bistro or local wine shop, you can always ask the manager for their used corks. The chances are good that they don't save any corks. Also, check with any local restaurants you know that serves wine. You can also look online. Sometimes you can find them on various online auction sites and get them for practically nothing. If you have friends that drink wine too, find out what they do with their corks. Combine your corks, have a wine cork craft party and choose a theme for your party!

CORK CRAFTING

*With just a little time and patience
you can create some very nice and
useful things*

There are many other uses a cork can serve besides keeping the wine in the bottle. What do you do with your corks after the bottle is empty? Do you save your corks but not sure why? This crafty cork manual will not only show you what you can do with the corks you already have but also give you ideas for using all the future corks you will have.

Before you Begin

Be sure to get together everything you will need by reading the **What You Need** section located within each cork craft project you are about to create. When using any tools or any sharp objects, be sure to take your time and take every safety precaution for the tool you are using. Common items needed to create most of the projects in this book are simply corks, glue gun, and glue but each project will be different and require its own set of items. You should be sure that you have all the necessary items for the project before you begin any construction on the project.

Each project also has an estimated time of construction from start to finish. This is especially good for determining which project to do when you are on a time budget.

Easy Refrigerator Magnets

These magnets are super easy to put together and they are also very useful and will be seen for years to come! They are creative, useful, and unique!

WHAT YOU NEED:
- Glue Gun (If necessary)
- Glue (If needed)
- Knife
- Gloves (recommended)
- Cutting Board
- 3 Button Magnets
- 1 Cork
- Paint (optional)

Estimated Time:
- 5 minutes or less

First, lay a cork down sideways on the cutting board. Next, cut it in half short ways into 3 pieces as close in measurement as possible with each other.

When you have the three pieces, you are ready to apply the button magnets.

Button magnets can be found at just about any hobby or craft store. Some button magnets come with an adhesive backing already attached to the magnet. This adhesive backing is really nice and makes the project even easier. The button magnets I used had the adhesive backing to them. If that's the case with you, peel off the protective backing on the button magnet and apply it to the top of one of the cork end pieces you cut.

Place one of the pieces you cut standing up on the cutting board. Even up the magnet with the cork and apply the adhesive to the side that has been cut. This leaves the opposite side nice and original looking. If you are using the middle piece that has both ends cut, choose the best looking side and place the magnet on the opposite side you chose. This will keep the best looking side as the side that will be seen. Apply some pressure for a moment to ensure the magnet is securely attached to the cork.

If the magnet does not have an adhesive backing, then apply some glue to the top of a standing cork piece on the cut end and attach the magnet to the cork. Allow a minute or two to dry. Once it has set up, you're done! Keep it looking original or paint it and add your own personal touch!

Cool Picture Frame

Make a cool and unique picture frame that will stand out wherever it is displayed! This cool cork frame will roughly allow any picture up to 3 ½ inches x 3 ¾ inches. The corks you are using could change the opening dimensions of the frame depending on their size.

WHAT YOU NEED:
🖉 Glue Gun
🖉 Glue
🖉 24 Corks
🖉 Cardboard 6 ¼" x 6 ¼"
Estimated Time:
⏲ 25 minutes

Begin by standing a cork up on the table.

Apply some glue to the top of the cork and place another cork standing up and on top of the cork you just applied the glue to. You should now have two corks that are standing up and glued together.

 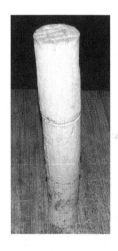 

Again, apply some glue to the top of the cork and place another cork that is standing up, on top of the two corks already glued together. Once more, apply some glue to the top of the cork and place a cork, standing up and on top of the three corks already glued together. You should now have four corks, all standing up and all attached on top of one other.

This will be used for the side of the frame. Four of these pieces will be needed, meaning you need to make three more pieces like the one you just made. After all four pieces are made it is time to create the top and bottom of the frame

Start by taking a cork and lying it down on the table so that one of the ends is pointing towards you. Place another cork in the exact same direction and up against the body of the cork you already placed on the table.

Firmly hold the two corks together and align the corks so that they are even on both ends. Using your glue gun, apply some glue in between the two corks to allow the corks to bond together. Allow a minute or so to dry, then flip over the piece and apply glue in between the corks for extra strength.

Place another cork the exact same way, up against the other corks and even with the cork ends, and hold into place. Once again, apply some glue in between the corks and bond them together. Allow a minute or so to dry, then flip over the piece and apply glue in between the corks. Finally, place one more cork the exact same way and against the body of the three corks already glued together. Be sure the ends are even with each other. Hold the corks firmly in place and against each other. Using your glue gun, apply glue in between the corks so that they are bonded together. Allow a minute or so to dry, then once again, flip over the piece and apply glue in between the corks to add more strength to the piece.

You should now have four corks, all pointing the same direction, and all attached to the body of each other. This will be the top of the frame. You will need to create another one just like this one to make the bottom of the frame. So once again, create one more piece consisting of four corks all attached to one another at the body, like the one you just created. This will be for the bottom of the frame. Once you have created the top and bottom of the frame, you are ready to put the frame together.

Begin by taking one of the side pieces and placing it up against the left side of the top piece you created so that the body of both cork pieces is touching together and the ends are even with each other.

Carefully hold the pieces together in place. Using your glue gun, apply some glue in between pieces to bond the top and left side together. Allow a minute or so to dry then take another side piece and place it up against the right side of the top piece. Hold the pieces together and apply some glue in between the two pieces. Again, allow a minute or so to dry.

Now it's time to attach the bottom piece. Take the bottom piece and place it in between the sides so that the corks are all touching each other. Firmly hold the corks together one end at a time and apply some glue in between the corks to bond them together.

Allow a minute or two to dry. Now you still have two side pieces that need to be added. Each one of these pieces will go on the outside of the existing side piece.

One will go on the left side and one will go on the right side. Place the side pieces up against the existing side so that all the corks are pointing the same. Carefully hold the pieces together and using your glue gun, apply glue between the two pieces from one end of the piece to the other end. After both the side pieces have been attached and glued together. Flip the frame over and add glue to the areas where you attached the pieces together. This will only add more stability to the frame.
 Before you attach the frame backing to the frame, you should inspect the frame to determine which side of your corks looks the best. The best side will be the

front side of the frame. Once you have determined the front side of the frame, it is time to attach the frame backing. Lay the frame down on the table with the front side facing the table and the back side pointing up. Take the custom cardboard piece you cut and add a thick coating of glue around the perimeter of the cardboard. This will be your frame backing and will go on the back of the frame. Using the cardboard, attach the backing to the back side of the frame carefully and making sure the glue will be attaching to all the sides, top and bottom.

This will also add more stabilization to all the corks. After the backing has dried, go back over and add any necessary glue between the cardboard backing and the frame. Allow a few minutes to dry and you're frame will be completed! Congratulations you're now ready to add a picture to your frame!

It's universal and looks great however you choose to display it! Since it is universal, determine which way you would like to display the frame. You can add a small eyebolt in the top center of the frame after you determine which side will represent the top of the frame. Or you can add a small hook on the cardboard backing. You can purchase a picture hanging kit for just a few dollars that will have an assortment of items you can use to hang your cool picture frame. The easiest way to hang it is with some heavy duty double-sided tape.

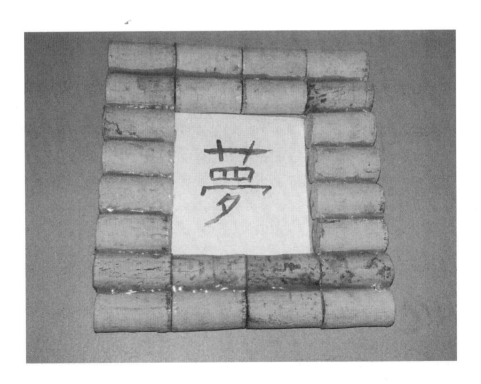

NIFTY TABLE TRIVET

There are many ways you can create a trivet using corks. This also makes a nice coaster as well! Start by doing the following: Using a knife, Lay a cork down on its side onto the cutting board and carefully cut the cork in half short ways approximately one third of the way down the cork. Now take this cut piece and place it up next to the remaining cork.

WHAT YOU NEED:

- Glue Gun
- Glue
- Knife
- Gloves
- Cutting Board
- 7 Corks
- Flat File or Fine Sand Paper

Estimated Time:
- 30 minutes

You will want to cut the remaining cork in half short ways also but it needs to be the same measurement as the piece you just cut.

You want each piece to be the same in measurement so your trivet will be level on top. Cut 6 more corks into thirds just like you did the first one. If any of the corks are a little uneven, take a flat file or some fine sand paper and gently go across the bottom of the cork. Compare the cork pieces to determine that they are all the same measurement. If the cork pieces are not all the same measurement, the trivet will not be level. It is very important that the trivet is level. You can level the trivet later after it is constructed. Save the shavings from the corks cut and evened because they will be needed later. After all the corks are cut into thirds, you are ready to glue all the pieces together.

Start with one piece standing up on the table and take another piece standing up and place it against the left side of the first piece or starting piece. Using your glue gun, carefully glue the pieces together. You will be placing each piece standing up and completely around the first cork you started with forming a circular pattern. Continue to stand each piece up beside the previous piece and touching the starting cork, gluing each piece carefully in place and in a circular pattern until a complete circle around the starting cork has been made.

It doesn't have to be a perfect circle. You should have around 6 cork pieces surrounding the starting cork. After the circle has been formed around the starting cork, allow the trivet to set up for a few minutes.

Next, you will want to create another circle around the circle you just created. So just like you have been doing, take a cork piece and lay it up against the body of one of the outer corks.

Using your glue gun, apply some glue in between the pieces to secure the pieces together. Again, continue the process with each cork piece until you have completed the circle. If there are any gaps in between the corks, this is where you will use the shavings saved from earlier. First add a little glue to the gaps, and then sprinkle some shavings over the glue to help cover and conceal the gaps. This will also make the trivet look nicer and give it a cleaner look. Test the trivet by placing a skillet or pan on it to ensure it is level or close enough to being level. It doesn't have to be perfect. If the trivet is not as level and needs to be trimmed up, gently take a flat file or fine sand paper and go over the entire trivet. Try not to take off too much at once and be sure you are doing it gently or otherwise it could all come apart. Keep the trivet on the table if you do have to level it any and be careful not to scratch up the table in the process. It would be safest to have the trivet on a cutting board the entire time. It's better if the flat file or fine sandpaper being used is larger than the trivet so you can level it more easily. This is because you're able to go across the entire trivet all at once. Once the trivet is level, you're done and ready to put it to use!

Optional

If you would like the trivet to be larger than cut more pieces out of full corks and add a third circle layer of pieces around the last circle you just made.

Distinctive Wine Rack

WHAT YOU NEED:
✏ Glue
✏ Glue Gun
✏ Small Coffee Can Lid or Small Lid
✏ 138 Corks
Estimated Time:
🕒 1 ½ Hours

A very unique piece of art that will stand out for sure! Creating this wine rack will definitely add an eye attraction wherever it ends up! This rack will hold 3 bottles of wine.

Begin by taking a small coffee can lid and placing it on the table.

Place it so that the rim of the lid is pointing towards the ceiling. If you don't have a coffee lid any kind of lid will work as long as the lid is larger in diameter than a wine bottle. I used a coffee lid from a small 10-12oz coffee can. The diameter of the coffee can lid I used was 4 inches. A standard wine bottle is around 3 inches. This gives the bottle plenty of room to fit inside the wine rack without any problems. Next take a cork and stand it up against the front of the coffee can lid. Take another cork and stand it up against the lid and also against the left side of the cork that is already standing.

Carefully press the corks together and using your glue gun, apply some glue in between the corks to bond them together. As with all the projects in this book, it's better to do this project with a cutting board or cardboard under the coffee can lid and the corks so that you don't get any glue on the table. Allow a minute to dry. Now take another cork, stand it up, and place it against the lid and against the left side of the last cork you attached. Make sure the lid is kept in place when each cork is added. If the lid tries to move around when you are applying the corks then place something on the lid to weight it down and keep it from moving.

You will be going completely around the coffee can lid attaching corks until the corks meet up with each other. So, carefully take another cork and place it next to and on the left side of the three corks already glued together and using your glue gun, apply some glue in between the corks to bond this piece in place. You should now have four corks all standing and all glued to the body of one another. Next take another cork, stand it up, and once again place it against the lid and against the left side of the attached corks. With your glue gun, apply some glue to secure this piece in place. Do not glue the pieces to the coffee can lid or the table! It's a very delicate and timely process of adding the glue so take your time on each piece you add. Before you add anymore corks, take your glue gun and apply glue in between each piece on the opposite side and the side that is facing the coffee can lid.

Now take another cork, stand it up and place it on the left side of the five corks already attached. Using your glue gun, apply glue in between the pieces just like you have done on all the pieces. Again, take another cork and stand it up. Place it against the left side of the last cork you just attached and repeat these processes until you have gone completely around the coffee can lid and the corks are meeting back up with your starting cork. It should be about 18 corks total surrounding the lid. That is assuming you are using a small coffee can lid about 4 inches in diameter. Remember that the circle you are creating has to be slightly larger than the wine bottle that will be going inside it. Remove the coffee can lid when you are done gluing the last piece.

Now, carefully examine over the piece and add any glue to places that look like they made need it. You want the piece to be as strong as possible. Once the piece is dry, using your glue gun, go around the inside of the attached corks and apply glue in between every piece. This will strengthen the piece and make it more durable. If you can't get the glue in between corks all the way, flip over the piece and apply glue in between all the pieces that look like they need it. When you are finished, allow a few minutes for the piece to dry. You should have a ring of corks that are all attached together at the body and all the corks are standing up. There should be a total of 18 corks used. You will need to create 3 of these pieces since each piece will be used for each bottle holder on the wine rack. Once all three pieces have been created, lay these pieces aside and you can now move along with the project.

Take one of the ring pieces you just created and place it on the table with the corks standing up. Now, using your glue gun apply some glue to the top of one of the corks closest to you. Next, take a cork, stand it up, and place it on the top the cork you applied the glue to. Even up the corks with each other. You are going to be adding a second layer of corks on top of and just like the first layer. Using your glue gun, apply some glue to the top of another cork on the cork piece.

Take a cork and place it on top of the cork you just applied the glue to. Even up the corks with each other. Repeat this process until you have gone completely around the piece and a second layer is added. After all 18 pieces have been added, take your glue gun and apply glue in between all the corks to help bond the second layer better. Also, add glue in between the corks inside the circle the best you can. This will only help bond the piece even more securely. You should have a circle of corks consisting of two layers. The corks should all be standing up and on top of one another.

The next step will involve a repeat of the last step. You will be adding a third layer. With your glue gun, apply some glue to the top of one of the corks closest to you. Now, take a cork and stand it up. Place it on top of the cork that you applied the glue to. Even up the corks with each other. Since you are applying a third layer to this piece, repeat the process until all 18 corks have been attached.

After all 18 corks are securely attached carefully apply glue in between all the cork pieces. Also apply glue in between all the corks inside the circle the best you can. You should now have 3 layers of corks consisting of 18 corks on each layer with a total of 54 corks.

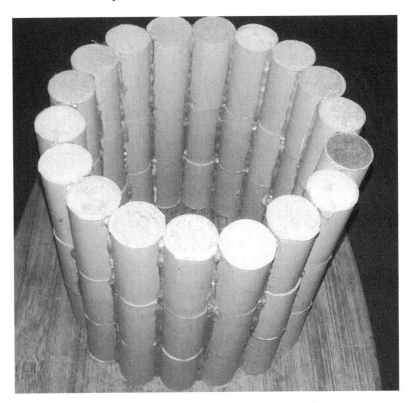

This piece will represent one bottle holder and since this wine rack holds 3 bottles, you will need to create 2 more pieces exactly like this one. Using the ring pieces you created at the beginning of this project, repeat the process with each ring piece and create 2 more pieces exactly like this piece you just created. Each of the 3 pieces should consist of the same amount of corks and should look identical. Once all 3 pieces have been created, it is time to move on with the project.

You are almost ready to assemble the wine rack however you will need to create one more piece. Take a cork and stand in up on the table so that the cork end is pointing towards the ceiling. Next, using your glue gun, apply some glue to the top of the standing cork. Take another cork, stand it up the same, and place it on top of the cork you applied the glue on.

Once more, apply some glue to the top of the standing corks with your glue gun then place another cork on top of the standing corks. You should now have three corks all standing up and all on top of each other. You now have all the pieces needed to assemble the wine rack.

Take one of the bottle holders and place it lying down on the table and with all the corks pointing towards you. Take another bottle holder, lay it down on the table the exact same way, and place it up against the other bottle holder. Place it so that the two bottle holder pieces are touching together and hold the piece firmly in place.

Using your glue gun, apply some glue in between the two cork pieces where they are joining. Allow the piece to dry for a minute and try to hold the piece firmly in place during that time to allow the pieces to bond together good. Once the pieces are bonded together, flip the piece over and with your glue gun, apply glue in between the pieces to strengthen the piece more. Allow a minute or so to dry.

Now you will be using the piece you just created consisting of 3 corks. Take this piece, lay it down so that the end of the cork piece is pointing towards you, and place it on top of, and in between the two bottle holders. Place it so that this piece is touching both of the bottle holder pieces. Even up the ends of 3 cork piece with the ends of the bottle holder piece. Hold the 3 cork piece firmly in place. Using your glue gun, apply some glue in between the corks on both sides of 3 cork piece to bond the bottle holder even better. Allow a minute or so to dry.

Finally, take your remaining bottle holder piece and place it on top of, and in the middle of two bottle holder piece. Place it so that the corks are all pointing towards you just like the two bottle holder piece. Even up the ends of the bottle holder piece with the ends of the two bottle holder piece. Hold the piece firmly in place.

Using your glue gun, apply some glue in between where the one bottle holder piece meets the two bottle holder piece. The piece should be bonded to both of the two bottle holders since it is on top of both bottle holders and also in the middle of both bottle holders. Now with your glue gun, apply an adequate amount of glue in between the front corks where the three bottle holders are all meeting each other. Turn the piece around and again apply some glue in between where the three bottle holders are all meeting each other. Carefully examine over the entire piece and apply additional glue where it needs it. Congratulations on your cool unique wine rack!

Effective Drink Coasters

WHAT YOU NEED:
- Glue
- Glue Gun
- 8 Corks

Estimated Time:
- 6 minutes

Making these simple drink coasters will add protection to your table while creating a unique touch! These also can make great gifts! They are super easy to make and are very useful all around the house. Synthetic corks work the best! Synthetic corks are more similar in dimensions with each other and work better for the coasters in my opinion. They are not required, however, so if you don't have synthetic corks real corks will be fine. This project teaches you how to make one simple drink coaster. There are several different cork designs you can use to create additional coasters. You will see several different types of drink coasters. The first type is the easiest to create.

Start by taking a cork and standing it up on the table.

Apply some glue with the glue gun to the top of the cork and place another cork, also standing up, on top of the standing cork you added the glue to. You should have two standing corks that are glued to each another. One cork should be standing on top of the other cork.

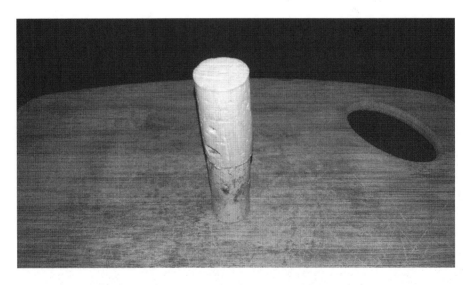

Place this piece aside and create three more pieces just like this piece. You need to create a total of four of these pieces. Each piece consists of two corks glued at the ends.

Once all four pieces are created, it's time to put the pieces together. Take one of the pieces and lay it down on the table so that the cork end is pointing towards you. Now take another piece and lay it down next to and against the body of the other piece that is already lying down.

The two pieces should be lying down the same direction and touching the body of each other. Next, using the glue gun, apply a sufficient amount of glue in between the two pieces from one end and all the way to the other end so that they will bond securely and hold together.

Be sure the ends are even with one another. Add another piece which will also be lying down and glue this piece next to and against the two pieces already glued together. Again, add a sufficient amount of glue in between the pieces to bond them securely. Finally, lay the last piece down, against and next to the other three pieces already glued together. Add glue in between the pieces from one end to the other. You just created one coaster and you are almost done! Carefully flip over the coaster over and apply glue in between all the pieces from end to end. This will make it stronger and will allow it to last longer.

Optional Designs

There are various ways to create your coaster. Add your own design, pattern, or texture to give it what it needs!

Single Wine Bottle Holder

What better way to store your wine bottle than in your unique cork wine holder! Start by taking a cork and standing it up on the table.

WHAT YOU NEED:
- Glue
- Glue Gun
- 98 Corks

Estimated Time:
- 1 Hour 20 Minutes

With your glue gun, apply glue to the top of the cork. Take another cork and stand it up and place it on top of the cork you applied the glue to. You should have two corks standing up and one cork should be standing on top of the other cork.

This will represent one piece. You are going to need 40 more pieces exactly like the one you just made. I know this seems like a lot but these are quick and easy to make. You can make several of these at one time since they are easy enough. A total of 41 pieces are needed and you have just created one piece. So, create 40 more of these pieces and then you will be ready to move on with everything.

After all 41 pieces have been made; you are ready to move on with the project! Much of the remaining portion of this project will consist of using the 41 pieces you created.

Now, take one of the pieces you just created and lay it down on the table with the cork end pointing towards you.

Take another piece and lay it down exactly the same way and against the body of the piece you just laid down. Press the two pieces together and even the ends of both pieces with one another. Hold the pieces in place and using your glue gun, apply an adequate amount of glue in between the two pieces. Add glue from one end of the corks to the other end to bond them together. Allow a minute or so to dry, flip over the piece, then apply glue in between the pieces from one end to the other just like you did on the other side.

Now, take another piece and lay it down with the cork pointing towards you and the same way as the other two pieces. Place the piece beside and against the body of one of the pieces you just glued. Firmly hold the corks together and using your glue gun, apply a sufficient amount of glue in between the pieces. Be sure the ends are all even with each other. You should now have three pieces all glued together at the body and all the corks should be even with each other. Allow it to dry and take one more two cork piece and lay it down just like the other pieces already attached. Place the piece against the body just like you did the other two and even the ends up with each other. Firmly hold both pieces together and apply glue in between the corks from one end to the other.

You should now have four cork pieces that are all glued to the body of each other. There should be a total of 8 corks used in this piece. All the ends of the corks should be even with each other. Allow a minute or so to dry and flip the entire piece over. Apply glue in between all four of the pieces just like you did the other side to help strengthen the cork. After the glue has been applied, lay this piece to the side. You will need to make four more of these pieces. Exactly like the one you just created. So repeat the process of the piece you just made here until you have a total of 5 pieces. You should have 5 cork pieces and each cork piece should consist of 8 corks all glued together and attached to each other. These five pieces will be used for two sides and the bottom of the wine cork holder. One piece will be used for the bottom of the holder and the other four pieces will be used for two of the sides. Two pieces will be used on one side and the other two pieces will be used on the opposite side.

Next you will begin the construction on the remaining two sides. These sides will be slightly larger than the other sides and will be constructed the same way using the two cork pieces you created at the beginning of this project. The construction is similar. Take a two cork piece and lay it down on the table with the cork end pointing towards you.

Take another piece and lay it down exactly the same way and against the body of the piece you just laid down. Press the two pieces together and even the ends of both pieces with one another. Hold the pieces in place and using your glue gun, apply an adequate amount of glue in between the two pieces. Add glue from one end of the corks to the other end to bond them together. Allow a minute or so to dry, flip over the piece, then apply glue in between the pieces from one end to the other just like you did on the other side.

Now, take another piece and lay it down with the cork pointing towards you and pointing the same way as the other two pieces that are bonded together. Place the piece up against the body of one of the pieces you just glued. Firmly hold the corks together and using your glue gun, apply a sufficient amount of glue in between the pieces. Be sure the ends are all even with each other. You should now have three pieces all glued together at the body and all the corks should be even with each other. Allow it to dry for a minute and then take another two cork piece and lay it down just like the other pieces already attached. Place the piece against the body the same way you did the other three pieces and even the ends up with each other. Firmly hold both pieces together and apply glue in between the corks from one end to the other. This gives you four cork pieces all glued at the body of each other and resembles the side pieces you made earlier.

The piece is not done yet. Again, take another one of the two cork pieces and lay it down with the cork pointing towards you and pointing the same way as the other four cork pieces glued together. Firmly hold the pieces in place and using your glue gun, apply glue in between the cork pieces just like you did the other pieces. Finally, take one last piece and place it up against the previous piece you just glued. Even the end with the others and firmly hold the pieces in place. Using your glue gun, add some glue in between the pieces from one end to the other. When you have finished, allow a minute or two to dry. Now, flip over the piece and apply any glue in between the corks that may need it. This is only adding to the stability of the holder. You should have 6 cork pieces all glued together with all the cork ends even with one another. This piece consists of 12 corks total. This will be one of the side pieces.

You now have one side piece made but this project requires 4 side pieces. So, using the remaining cork pieces you made at the beginning of this project, create 3 more pieces exactly like the one you just finished creating. Once you have completed and have 4 side pieces, you will be ready to assemble the wine cork holder.

Now that you have all the pieces you need, you are ready to put them all together. You should have 5 eight cork pieces and 4 twelve cork pieces. The four twelve cork pieces will be used for the two of the sides and four eight cork pieces will be used for the other two sides. One eight cork piece will be used for the bottom piece. Begin by taking one of the twelve cork pieces and standing it up on the table so that the cork ends are pointing upwards and facing the ceiling. Now take an eight cork piece and stand it up and place it against the first row of corks on the twelve cork piece. Place the eight cork piece in front of and against the first row of corks on the row farthest left on the twelve cork piece. Place the eight cork piece in front of the twelve cork piece and not on the outside of it. Carefully hold the two pieces in place and using your glue gun, apply glue all along and in between where the cork pieces meet. Give it a few minutes to dry before continuing with the project.

Now take another twelve cork side and place it standing up against and on the outside of the eight cork piece you just attached. The corks on the opposite end should look like they will meet up once the next piece goes in place. Before you place the next piece in place, add any extra glue necessary to the insides of where the pieces meet. Once the last piece goes in, you may not be able to access those areas anymore.

Take an eight cork piece and stand it up on the table. Place this piece in between the open side of the pieces to close in the square. Line the corks up with each side. Using your glue gun, apply an adequate amount of glue in between the pieces on both sides of where they meet up with the other corks.

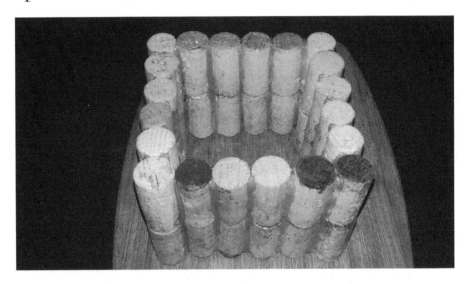

You should now have a square box without any bottom. It is now a good time to install the bottom piece while you still can access it. Take an eight cork piece and place it inside the box so that it meets up with the inside of all four sides. Place the piece inside the box the best way it fits. Try not to force the piece in if the piece can be rotated to fit better. You may have to flip over the eight cork piece or rotate it to find the best way it will position inside the box. Once you have determined how the piece will go inside the box, carefully push the piece inside and to the bottom of the box. Lift the box off the table and check underneath it to make sure the corks are all even and aligned with one another. Using your glue gun, apply some glue in between the sides and the bottom piece to bond the pieces together. Allow a minute or so to dry and then place the holder on the table. Using your glue gun, carefully apply glue inside the box and where the sides meet up with the bottom piece. You will have gaps between the bottom piece and the sides so after the glue you applied has dried, it may be a good idea to go back over the bottom piece and add any additional glue where necessary to fill in the gaps as best as possible.

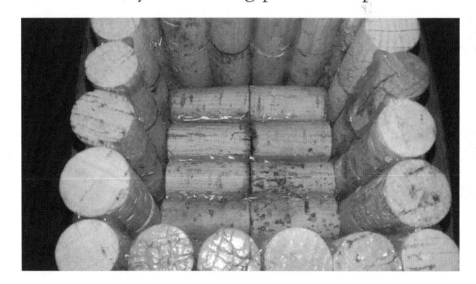

Now using your glue gun, apply glue along the top of all the corks on the back side of the holder. Take a twelve cork piece, stand it up, and place it on top of the corks you just applied the glue on. Even the two pieces up the best you can. Apply glue on both sides and in between where the two pieces meet up. Allow a minute to dry and then take your glue gun and apply glue along the top of the left side of the corks. Take an eight cork piece, stand it up, and place it on top of the left corks you just applied the glue on. Even the two cork pieces up the best you can.

Again, apply glue on both sides where the two corks meet up and then allow a minute to dry. Now using your glue gun, apply glue along the tops of the corks on the right side of the holder. Take the last eight cork piece, stand it up, and place it on top of the right corks you applied the glue on.

Once again, apply some glue on both sides and in between where the two cork pieces meet up and allow a minute or so to dry. For the last time, apply glue along the tops of the corks that are in the front. Take the twelve cork piece, stand it up, and place it on top of the corks your just applied the glue on.

Take your glue gun and apply glue on both sides where the two cork pieces meet up. Allow a minute or so to dry and examine the holder for any places that may need additional glue. Once you have filled in the areas that needed additional glue, allow a few minutes to dry. Congratulations on your new wine bottle holder!

Aquarium Sailboat

WHAT YOU NEED:
- Scissors
- Knife
- Gloves
- Cutting Board
- Toothpick
- White Paper
- 1 Cork
- Ruler (optional)

Estimated Time:
- 5 minutes

It is time for you to create your very own sailboat! Quick and easy to build! A sailboat that will float and sail anytime! Start by laying a cork down on its side on a cutting board.

Lay the cork with the ends pointing left to right. Hold the cork firmly in place and using your knife, cut the cork in half short ways. Next, stand up one of the two cork pieces that you just cut and it doesn't matter which one you use.

Now, using your knife cut the piece in half down the middle.

Take a toothpick and cut it in half with your scissors. Using the pointed end of one of the toothpick pieces, poke a hole in the center of one of the cork pieces you just cut in half down the middle. Again, it doesn't matter which piece you choose to use. Stick the toothpick deep enough in the center of the cork to secure the toothpick in place. Remove the toothpick piece you used to create the hole. Now, use the other toothpick piece and insert the toothpick in the cork with the pointed end facing up and the end you cut inserted in the cork. It's time to add the sails! Using scissors cut out a small square from some white paper or whatever color you would like. Computer paper works great but any kind of paper will work. Cut the paper about 1¾ by 1¾ inch. I gently tore mine to give it a more unique and rustic appearance. After you have the paper cut, its ready to be placed on the sailboat. Gently fold the paper in half and poke a hole through the top center of the folded paper so that it goes through both halves.

Go through the folded paper about a ¼ inch from where the ends meet and about the halfway point for the sides. Finally, carefully pull or space the two halves apart from each other to form your sails. Your sailboat is ready to set sail!

Detailed Model Airplane

WHAT YOU NEED:
🖉 Scissors
🖉 Knife
🖉 Gloves
🖉 Cutting Board
🖉 Glue Gun
🖉 Glue
🖉 Toothpick
🖉 2 Corks
🖉 Ruler (optional)
Estimated Time:
🕒 10 minutes

Build a creative detailed airplane with only two corks! Start by laying a cork down on its side onto a cutting board.

Next, using your knife cut the cork in half short ways.

Next, stand up one of the pieces you just cut (it doesn't matter which piece) and cut it in half right down the middle.

These two half-circle pieces will be the wings. The other half cork will be used to create the propeller and tail after the wings are attached. However, for now lay a full cork down on the table. Take one of the wings and with your glue gun, apply some glue to the cut end of the half-circle pieces you just cut and attach it to the middle of and on the side of the full cork. Attach the piece with the cut side facing down and halfway in between both sides of the full cork and halfway up the cork so that the wing is not resting on the table. Take the other half-circle piece and do the same thing to the other side. Apply some glue to the cut end of the piece and attach it to the other side of the full cork. Again, apply the piece halfway in between the cork with the side you cut facing downward. Both pieces should line up with one another but one should be attached to one side of the full cork and the other piece should be attached to the other side of the full cork.

After the wings are dry it is time to add the propeller, tail, cock pit, and landing gear! We will start with the propeller. Get the half cork piece that was first cut in half. Lay the cork on its side. With a knife, cut the cork in half short ways about a ¼ inch from one of the ends. This piece should look like a wheel. Lay the wheel piece down and cut it in half down the middle.

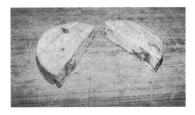 

Try to make the cut as straight as possible. Now take one of those pieces and carefully cut it down the middle long ways. You now have the cock pit and propeller for your airplane. Using scissors carefully cut a small piece off a toothpick about ¼ inch or so in length. Insert one end of the toothpick into the end of the airplane cork body.

Whichever end you want to represent the front of the plane. Place the toothpick in the center of the cork. Next, insert the middle of the cork propeller into the toothpick you just installed. You now have the propeller installed!

Now, take the other half wheel piece that you have leftover from making the propeller. Apply some glue to the cut end with your glue gun. Next, place this piece in between the wings of the airplane and on top of the cork body of the airplane. Allow a moment to dry before continuing. You just created the cock pit to the airplane.

Now, take the other half wheel piece you have and carefully cut it in half short ways down the middle. This piece should be a little smaller than the cock pit you just added.

Apply some glue to the smaller one of the triangular pieces and attach the piece at the end of the airplane body and on top of the airplane. The tallest point of the triangle piece should be facing up and glue applied to the bottom of the piece. The piece should be on top of the cork and in the middle of the cork but at the end of the cork and behind the wings.

It's time to install the landing gear. Using scissors cut two small pieces about ¼ of an inch in length off a toothpick. Make sure these pieces are about the same in measurement. Poke one toothpick piece halfway down the cork on the bottom side of the airplane body at a 45 degree angle. Poke the other piece halfway down and on the bottom of the cork at a 45 degree angle on the other side. You can now turn the airplane over.

The toothpick pieces should allow the airplane to have a slight tilt upward, keeping the wings and propeller off the ground and giving it a better display. Paint the model airplane to give it a more personal touch!

Super Simple Model Car

WHAT YOU NEED:	
✏	Glue Gun
✏	Glue
✏	Knife
✏	Gloves
✏	Cutting Board
✏	Scissors
✏	Toothpick or Bamboo Skewer
✏	2 Corks
✏	Ruler (optional)
Estimated Time:	
🕑	8 minutes

This car is very easy to make and will look nice next to your miniature sailboat and airplane. Start by laying a cork down on its side on a cutting board.

Cut the cork in half short ways with a knife about a ¼ inch off the end of the cork. Next, use this piece you just cut as a template and cut 4 more just like this template.

Cut the remaining four pieces from the same cork. These will be used for the wheels of the car. The template piece will be used for the top of the car. Once all the pieces are cut it is time to create the axles. Take a toothpick and cut four small pieces of equal length or as close to equal length as possible. Cut each piece about a ¼ inch in size. They don't have to be exact. You will be evening them up when they go into the car body. After all of these pieces have been made, you are ready to create the top of the car.

Take the template for the wheels that you cut a minute ago and lay it down flat on the cutting board. Cut the template wheel right down the middle, creating two half circles. Now that all of the pieces have been made, it is time to assemble the car.

Lay a full cork down sideways and on each side of the cork, take a toothpick and poke a hole near both ends and a little lower than halfway down the cork. These holes are where the wheels will be going. Line the holes up on each side the best you can. You will want to repeat the process on the other side of the cork body. There should be four holes poked total, two on both sides. Don't poke the toothpick too far in the cork! A bamboo skewer works well for poking the holes. Poking the holes ahead of time only makes it easier for the small toothpick pieces to go in. Once all the holes have been made, you can now start to assemble the car. Take the four small toothpick pieces and insert each one in the four holes of the cork. Leave enough of the toothpick out of the cork so that the wheel will fit on good.

Now before you place the wheels on, take a toothpick or bamboo skewer and poke a hole in the center of each wheel. Next, take the four wheels and carefully put each wheel on each of the four toothpick axles. After the wheels are attached, it is time to apply the top piece to the car.

Take the half circle template wheel (whichever half looks better but it doesn't matter which one you use) and apply some glue to the flat side or the side you cut. Align the piece with the top of the cork about halfway down the cork.

Apply the piece to the body of the car in between the front and back wheels. Place the piece so that the contoured ends of the top piece are pointing the same direction as the body of the car. After the top is applied, allow a minute to dry before showing all your friends your new car!

Floating Castaway Sailboat

WHAT YOU NEED:
- Scissors
- White or Colored Paper
- Cutting Board
- Glue Gun
- Ruler
- Glue
- Bamboo Skewer
- 3 Corks

Estimated Time: 5 minutes

If you created the miniature sailboat, then you will definitely want to add this one to your collection! This is really simple to make and it really floats! Start by taking a cork and laying it down on the cutting board.

Take another cork and lay it down the same way and against the body of the other cork. Carefully hold the two pieces together and with the glue gun, add glue in between each cork so they bond together.

Now, take another cork and lay it down the same way the other two corks are laid and against the body of other cork attached. Again, apply glue in between the pieces to bond them together. Allow a few minutes to dry, then flip the piece over and apply glue in between the pieces like you did the other side. You should now have three corks all lying down and all glued together. This will be the raft to the sailboat!

Next you will need your bamboo skewer. These are found in the craft store or your local grocery store should carry them also. They are typically used to make shish kabobs. Cut a bamboo skewer about 3 inches in length. Using the pointed end of the skewer, poke a small hole in the center of the middle cork. Once the small hole is made, insert the skewer with the pointed end inside the raft. Now it is time to attach the sails! Using your ruler, mark and create a rectangle 1 ½ inches wide by 3 inches long. Cut this piece out of whatever color you want the sails to be! Carefully cut the rectangle you just drew. Now take the cut paper and fold the paper in half.

Take your bamboo skewer and carefully poke a hole through the center of the folded paper and about ¼ of an inch down from the edge of the paper where the ends meet. Go through both halves and unfold the paper and the sails have been raised!

Add an extra touch by installing a small eye hook on the front or back of the sailboat. Tie some kite string or fishing twine to the eye ring and you're set. Now, you will have more control over the sailboat when you put it in the water and it will be ready to tie it off to shore when you're done!

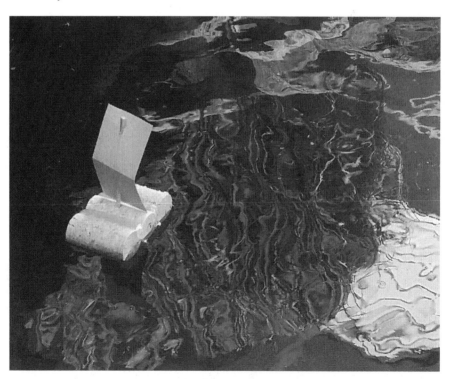

Fancy European Car Model

If you created the miniature car, the fancy car will only add to your collection! It looks great and is not hard to make! Start with the body of the car. Lay a cork down on its side on a cutting board and cut the cork in half short ways in the middle of the cork.

WHAT YOU NEED:

✎	Knife
✎	Cutting Board
✎	Glue Gun
✎	Glue
✎	Scissors
✎	toothpick
✎	Gloves
✎	2 Corks
Estimated Time:	
🕐	6 minutes

Next, take a full cork and stand it up on its end. Now, using the glue gun, apply glue to the top of the cork.

Attach one of the cork halves you just cut (It doesn't matter which one) to the top of the cork. The half cork should also be standing. Place the cork end that you cut to the top of the full cork you just applied glue to. You should now have a cork that's about 1 ½ times the size of a regular cork. This will be the body of the car. Now it is time to move on to creating the wheels for the car. Place another cork down on its side on a cutting board and cut the cork in half short ways about a quarter of an inch down from the end of the cork.

Using this piece just cut as a template, cut three more just like the template. After all four wheels are created; you are ready to make the axles to support each wheel in the body. Take a toothpick and using scissors cut four small pieces as close to each other in size as possible about ¼ inch. These four pieces will be used as the axles for the car. Once the axles are created, install the axles to the body.

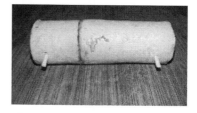

To do this, lay the body you created earlier down on its side. The body is the cork with the half cork glued to the end of it. On both sides of this piece, take a bamboo skewer or a toothpick and poke a small hole near both ends and just below the middle of the body. There should be a total of four holes poked, two on both sides. Don't poke the toothpick or bamboo skewer too far in the cork! Poking the holes ahead of time only makes it easier for the small toothpick pieces to go in.

Once all the holes have been poked, take the axles or the four small toothpick pieces cut earlier and insert each one in the four holes of the cork. Next take the four wheels and using a toothpick or bamboo skewer carefully poke a hole through the center of each wheel.

Once the center holes are poked in the wheels, attach all four wheels to the axles on the car. Once you have attached the wheels to the car its time to add the top of the car and some finishing touches to give it a fancier look. To create the top of the car, you will need the other cork piece that was cut in half short ways earlier.

Take the half cork piece and lay it down so the ends are pointing sideways. Using your knife cut the half cork down the middle and in half. Now, stand up one of the half pieces you just cut on its end on a cutting board.

Using a knife cut the cork in half down the middle of the cork. Take one of the pieces (it doesn't matter which one) and using the glue gun, apply some glue to the flat side of the piece. The flat side is the cut side. Attach the piece to the top of the car with the flat side down on the top of the body of the car. The top should be placed so that the cork end of the piece is pointing towards you.

Apply the piece in between the wheels and overlapping where the corks of the body meet.

Now it is time to add the front decal to finalize its look. Start by laying the other half circle cork piece you just cut down on its side and pointing sideways on a cutting board.

Place it so that the cut side is on the cutting board. Using a knife carefully cut the cork piece in half short ways about ¼ of an inch or smaller in size. After the half circle piece has been cut, take the piece and lay it on the cutting board and cut it down the middle but a little smaller than halfway on the piece.

Choose the smaller of the pieces and this is the front decal and will be applied on top of the car and near the front edge of the car.

Apply some glue to the small piece and attach the piece to the top of the car in between both wheels and with the point of the piece pointing towards the body of the car. Place it so that the contoured end of the piece is facing the front of the car. Allow a minute for the piece to dry and congratulations on creating your fancy car!

Civil War Cannon

Create a miniature civil war cannon very easily. First, begin by taking a cork and standing it up on a piece of scrap wood.

WHAT YOU NEED:

- Knife
- Marker or Pen
- Drill
- Gloves
- ¼ " Wood Drill Bit
- Cutting Board
- Scrap Wood
- Scissors
- toothpick
- 2 Corks

Estimated Time:
- 6 minutes

With your marker or pen, mark a dot in the middle of the cork. Using protective gloves, carefully carve out around the dot you marked with your knife. Make the outer rim of the hole slightly larger than your drill bit.

This is just to keep the bit from ripping or tearing the outside rim of the cork when you begin drilling. It will give the cannon a cleaner look!

Now, using a drill with a ¼ inch wood bit, carefully drill a hole in the center of the cork and drill down inside the cork about ½ inch. Take your time and be careful drilling into the cork. Be sure to keep the drill straight when drilling and keep your fingers clear of any danger. You won't have to apply much pressure so focus more on keeping the drill straight and in the center of the cork. It may be a good idea to wear gloves since you will be drilling downward and securing it with your fingers. This will be the cannon. After you have finished drilling it is time to move on to the next step.

Next, take another cork and lay it on its side on a cutting board. Using a knife carefully cut the cork in half short ways about ¼ of an inch in size. This is one of the wheels for the cannon.

You will need two wheels, so cut another piece in half short ways also ¼ of an inch in size. Now that both of the wheels have been created, take a toothpick and using scissors cut two pieces off the toothpick about ¼ of an inch in size. These will be the axles that will be used to attach the wheels to the cannon. Now you will attach the wheels to the cannon. To do this, lay the cannon down on its side and poke a small hole in the side of cannon opposite to the end you drilled out. Poke the hole on the side of, in the center of and near the end of the cork. Insert the small ¼ inch toothpick you cut with the scissors into the hole you poked in the side of cork.

Next take one of the wheels you cut earlier and find the center of the wheel. Poke a small hole in the center of the cork using your scrap toothpick. Now take the wheel and insert it on the axle and cannon. You should have a cannon with a wheel attached to the side facing you. Now rotate the cannon and add the wheel to the other side by again poking a small hole in the center of the cork near the end and parallel with the other wheel attached. You want the wheels to be aligned with each other as much as possible. After the hole is poked, Take the other ¼ inch toothpick cut and insert it into the hole you poked. Next, take the other wheel you cut earlier and locate the center of the wheel. Using the scrap toothpick, poke a small hole in the center of the wheel.

Insert the wheel in the toothpick axle on the cannon. Take your scissors and cut two more ¼ inch pieces from the scrap toothpick. After the pieces have been created, poke a small hole in the center, on top of the cork, and near the end of the cork side you drilled earlier. Insert the ¼ inch toothpick in the hole you poked. This is to represent the sights for the cannon.

Next, flip the cannon over on its back and poke another hole. Poke the hole in the center of the cork and on top of the cork near the end of the side that you drilled earlier. Insert the other ¼ inch toothpick you cut earlier.

This tilts the cannon up a little and represents a front stand for the cannon. Flip the cannon back over and you're done!

To be more creative, you can add a small wick to the back of the cannon and lay a couple BBs down next to the cannon to give it a more detailed look. Add the wick by poking a small hole on top of the cannon where the wheels are located. The hole should be poked in the middle of the cork and in between the wheels. Take a small piece of paper about ¼ of an inch in size. Twist the paper a few turns to give it more stability and to make it look more like a cannon wick. Insert the small piece of twisted paper in the hole you poked on top of the cannon.

Optional

Add a more realistic touch by painting the cannon. You can paint the wheels black and the cannon silver or whatever color you want!

Creative Birdhouse

This project requires a little more time and energy constructing, however, the results will make it well worth your time. It is easy to make and doesn't require any cutting or drilling. This will look great no matter where you decide to place it. It will add an eccentric look anywhere! This can also be the best gift for any occasion!

WHAT YOU NEED:	
✶	Glue Gun
✎	Glue
✎	211 Corks
Estimated Time:	
⏲	3 hours

Start by taking a cork and standing it up on your table or workbench. Add some glue to the top of the cork and place another cork, standing up, on top of the cork you just applied glue to.

You should now have two corks, both standing up and glued to one another. Next, add some glue to the top of the two standing corks and add a third cork, also standing up, on top of the other two corks. You now have three corks that are all glued together and standing on top of one another. This will represent one piece.

You need to create 52 of these pieces total. So, you need to make 51 more of the pieces like the one you just made. This will take a little while so allow yourself plenty of time to construct these pieces. You will also be creating a few other pieces but not until a little later. First, you need to create the 52 pieces before continuing to the next step in this project. After all 52 three-piece corks are created, you are ready to move on to the next step!

Now that you're ready to move on with the project it's time to make more a few more pieces that are going to be needed. Take a cork and lay it down on its side on the table so that the cork end is pointing towards you. Take another cork, lay it down, and place it the same direction and against the body of the other cork. Firmly hold the two pieces in place. Using your glue gun, apply some glue in between the two corks to bond them together. Apply the glue from one end of the corks to the other end. When finished, allow a minute to dry then flip the piece over. Apply glue in between the two corks just like you did on the other side. You have just created the next piece!

Since only 2 of these pieces are needed total, you're almost done with this part! You can lay this one aside and it will be used shortly. For now, make one more piece like the one just made here. Lay a cork down on its side with ends pointing towards you. Take another cork, lay it down, and place it the same direction and against the body of the other cork. Firmly hold the two pieces in place. Using your glue gun, apply some glue between the two corks to bond them together. Apply the glue from one end of the corks to the other end. When finished, allow a minute to dry then flip the piece over. Apply glue in between the two corks just like you did on the other side.

After both of these cork pieces are made, it is time to start the construction. You are going to be using these two pieces very soon, so keep them close. First, however, start by taking one of the 52 three-cork pieces that you made earlier and lay it down sideways on the table. Lay it down with the cork ends pointing sideways from left to right.

Take another one of the three-piece corks and lay it down the exact same way and up against the body of other three-cork piece. Firmly hold the two pieces together. Using your glue gun, apply an adequate amount of glue along the middle of the two pieces so that the glue is applied in between both pieces and from one end of the piece to the other end. Be sure the ends are as even with each other as possible. Try to make sure that the corks are all touching the body of one another and that enough glue is applied.

Now it is time to attach both the two-piece corks you just created a moment ago. You should currently have 2 three-piece corks lying down, sideways, ends even with one another, with both pieces attached and glued together.

Next, take one of the two-piece corks you made earlier, lay it down the exact same way as the other pieces, and place it against the left cork body of the three cork piece. Hold the pieces firmly together and using your glue gun, apply an adequate amount of glue to join the pieces together. Make sure the ends of the corks are even with one another. Take the remaining two-piece cork and lay it down the exact same way as the other pieces, and against the right cork body of the three cork piece. Once again, hold the pieces together and apply glue in between the pieces so they are attached to each other. Be sure the ends of the pieces are even with each other. You want both two-piece corks to be against the three-piece corks, one on the left side and one on the right side.

 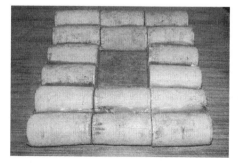

After the glue has dried, take another three-piece cork and lay it down with the corks in the same direction as the other attached pieces and against the two pieces you just attached. Hold the pieces firmly together and apply some glue in between the left and right corks to attach the pieces together. You won't be able to apply any glue in the middle because there is no cork there. Take another three-piece cork and lay it down the exact same direction and up against the three-piece you just attached. Once again, hold the pieces firmly together and apply glue in between the two pieces so they are attached together. Again, be sure the ends of the corks are all are flush or even with each other. You should now have a small square-shape piece that has a smaller square opening in the middle of it. There should be a total of 16 corks all attached together. This will be the front of the birdhouse and will be where the birds can access their home. Once this piece is dry, go back and apply additional glue in between all the corks touching one another to ensure more stability. When finished with one side, flip it over and again apply glue in between all the corks for maximum stability. You have completed the front of the birdhouse. You can lay the front piece aside and move on with the project!

Now you're ready to begin creating the sides and the bottom of the birdhouse! Creating the sides, the back, and the bottom are all going to be the same dimensions. All four pieces will be the exact same process.

Start by taking a three-cork piece and laying it down on the table sideways. Take another three-piece cork, also lying down sideways, and place it against the other piece. Hold the two pieces firmly together and apply some glue in between the two pieces from end to end. Next, take another three-piece cork and lay it down the exact same way as the other pieces and again hold the pieces firmly together and apply glue in between the pieces from end to end. As always, make sure the ends of the corks are flush and even with each other.

You should now have 3 three-piece corks all attached with the cork ends pointing sideways and all three cork pieces glued to one another. The cork pieces should all be lying down and all the pieces should be attached together. Now, take another three-cork piece and lay it down the exact same as the others and against the other piece. Hold the pieces firmly together and using your glue gun, apply some glue in between the two pieces from end to end. You should now have 4 three-piece corks lying down but all attached to each other and all the corks facing the same direction. All the ends of the pieces should be flush or even with one another.

Take another three-piece cork and lay it down the same way and against the other piece. Again, ensure the ends are even with one another and hold the pieces firmly together. Apply some glue in between the pieces from end to end. Take 1 more three-piece cork and lay it the same way and against the other piece. Hold the two pieces together and make sure the ends are even with each other. Apply some glue in between the cork pieces from end to end. You should now have 6 three-piece corks that are all lying down and all the pieces are lying down facing the same direction. It should consist of a total of 18 corks. It should consist of 3 columns and 6 rows. Go back over and apply additional glue in between all the corks to help securely bond the corks. Once the glue has been applied in between all the pieces and is dry, flip over the piece. Again, apply glue in between all the pieces to make the piece more stable.

Once you have applied enough glue, lay this piece over to the side with your front piece.

This piece will be used for the side, the back, or the bottom of the birdhouse. The sides, the back, and the bottom will each use one of these pieces. Four of these pieces need to be made total and you just created one piece. Three more pieces still need to be created before you can move on. Return to the top of this section and follow the instructions again to begin creating the remaining three pieces that will be needed.

Once all four pieces are created, you are ready to move on with the project. You should now have one front piece and 4 three-cork pieces consisting of 18 corks on each piece. These 4 pieces should be exactly the same as each other. The next pieces you are going to create are the roof of the birdhouse.

Take a three-piece cork and lay it down on the table sideways. Take another three-piece and lay it down on the table the same way as the other piece and against the body of the other piece you just laid down. Even the ends up and firmly hold the pieces together. Using your glue gun, apply some glue in between the corks from one end to the other end to ensure the pieces are bonded together.

Take another three-piece cork and again lay the piece sideways and against the last piece you just laid down. Using your glue gun, apply glue in between the pieces from one end to the other end. Repeat this process until you have a total of 10 three-piece corks all attached together, laying down sideways and pointing the same direction.

All the corks are facing sideways and the same direction with one another. All the ends are even with one another and they are all bonded together.

You will have a total of 30 corks used for this piece. It should consist of 10 three cork pieces all lying down with the cork ends pointing sideways. All the pieces should be glued together from one end of the piece to the other end. This piece will be used for one side of the roof.

The roof consists of two sides and both these need to be identical to each other. Each side of the roof uses 30 corks. So, you will need to go back to the beginning of this section and create one more piece consisting of 10 three-piece corks all attached together, facing the same direction, and all the cork ends as even with one another as possible. Create the piece exactly like the one you just made.

At this point, you should have: the front of the birdhouse, both sides, the bottom, the back, and both sides of the roof. It has taken you awhile to build these pieces but all your work will pay off soon! You are now going to start putting the pieces together and forming the birdhouse.

Start with the bottom piece. You can use any of the 4 pieces you made earlier that represent the sides, back, and the bottom. You are going to use all 4 of these pieces now.

Start by attaching the back of the birdhouse to the bottom of the birdhouse. Take 1 of the 4 pieces you made earlier and lay it on the table. This will be the bottom piece. Place it so that the cork ends are all pointing sideways. Now take another one of the 4 pieces and stand it up but with all the corks pointing sideways just like the bottom piece. Place it up against the backside of the bottom piece. The cork ends should all be pointing sideways on both pieces. Carefully and firmly hold the two pieces together so that the corks on the bottom row of the back piece is against the backside of the bottom cork piece already lying down. Make sure that the ends of both pieces are even with one another. Now using your glue gun, apply an adequate amount of glue between the cork pieces to attach the pieces together. Hold the pieces in place allowing a minute to dry before releasing the pieces and attaching the next piece.

After the piece has dried, Take another piece and stand it up but stand it up so that the cork ends are all pointing towards you. Carefully place this piece against the left side of the bottom piece that is lying on the table. Align the ends together with the bottom piece and just like the last piece. Carefully hold the two pieces together. Using your glue gun, apply glue in between the two pieces to attach them together. Carefully hold both pieces in place allowing a minute for them to dry before attaching the next piece. There will be a gap in the corner between the left piece you just attached and the back piece. This will be covered up later in the project so leave it for now.

At this point, you should have the bottom, back, and the left side all attached together. You should have one more side piece and the front piece left to be attached. You are going to attach the right side to the birdhouse first and leave the front piece for last. Take the remaining side piece and stand it up but stand it up so that the cork ends are all pointing towards you. Place the piece on the right side and against the bottom piece of the birdhouse. Even the ends up with the bottom piece and carefully hold the two pieces together. Using your glue gun, apply glue in between the two pieces so that they will be bonded with one another. Allow a minute or two to dry. Once again, don't worry about the gap in between the right piece and the back piece. They will be filled in later.

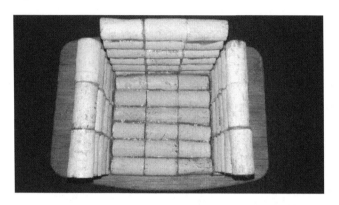

Now it is time to attach the front of the birdhouse. Take the front piece or the piece that has the opening in the middle of it and stand the piece up. Stand it up so that the ends are all pointing sideways and place the piece against the bottom of the birdhouse. Hold the two pieces together and using your glue gun, apply glue in between the two pieces to attach them together. Allow a minute or two to dry. Take the piece and flip it over.

Using your glue gun, apply glue in between all the areas where the bottom piece is attached to the other pieces. This will add more durability and strength to the birdhouse. After you have finished, allow a minute or two to dry before moving on.

Once the piece has dried, flip the piece back over and place it so the front of the birdhouse is facing you. You should have 4 three-piece cork pieces leftover that you haven't used yet. These 4 pieces are going to act as columns on each corner of the birdhouse. Take a three-piece cork and stand it up. Place the piece in between the cork ends on the front left side of the birdhouse.

The piece should be against the birdhouse and in between the ends of where both sides meet on the front left side of the birdhouse. Hold the piece firmly in place and using your glue gun, apply glue in between the pieces from top to bottom. Apply glue on both sides of the piece so that the piece will bond to both.

Take another three-piece cork, stand it up, and place it against the right side of the birdhouse. Place it against where both sides meet and firmly hold the piece in place. Using your glue gun, apply glue in between both sides of the piece to attach the piece with the birdhouse. Once you have finished, rotate the birdhouse 180 degrees and repeat the process of adding the columns to the back side of the birdhouse. Take another three-piece cork, stand it up, place it on the left side and against the birdhouse. Glue the piece in place and repeat the process with the right side of the birdhouse.

Once the columns have been installed, you are ready to move on with the project.

The birdhouse is almost complete and there are only a few more steps left! Lay the birdhouse to the side and grab some corks.

Once again you need to construct some more pieces that are going to be needed to finish this project. Take a cork and stand it up on the table. Using your glue gun, apply some glue to the top of the cork. Take another cork and stand it up on top of the cork you just applied glue to. Apply some glue to the top of the cork and place another cork, also standing up, on top of the other two standing corks. Apply some glue to the top of the cork and once more, place a cork, standing up, on top of the three corks that are already standing.

You now have four corks all attached together and all standing on top of one another. You will need to create 10 of these pieces total. You just created one piece so you only need to construct 9 more of these pieces.

After the 10 pieces have been made, you are ready to move on with the project. Start by taking the birdhouse placing it on the table and with the front of the birdhouse facing you. You will be using the 10 pieces you made to go along the top or ceiling of the birdhouse. Using your glue gun, apply glue along the top of the front side of the birdhouse. Only apply glue to the top left cork on the front side. Do not apply any glue on top of the column. Now, apply glue along the top of the back left cork on the birdhouse. Now, take one of the 10 pieces you just constructed and place it lying down but on top of the birdhouse so that one end of the piece is lying on top of the front side and the other end of the piece is lying on top of the back side.

 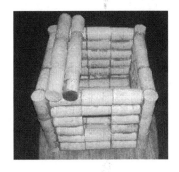

The cork end of the piece should be pointing towards you. Place the piece starting on the top left cork that you just applied glue on and align the piece so that the piece is on the left cork of both the front and back of the birdhouse. Six of these pieces will be used for the ceiling to the birdhouse. Now, take another piece and lay the piece down the same way and against the piece you just laid down. Apply any necessary glue to the other half of the top left cork if the glue has already dried. Repeat the process until you have 6 pieces, pointing towards you and lying down across the top of the birdhouse. This will represent the ceiling of the birdhouse and is also needed for supporting the roof.

Once all 6 pieces are down, using your glue gun apply glue in between the cork pieces to bond them all together and to make the structure more solid.

Take another four piece cork and lay it down the same way as the corks you just applied, and then place the piece on top of and in between the 3rd and 4th cork pieces of the ceiling. This is the middle of the ceiling no matter which side you count from. Using your glue gun, apply some glue on both sides of the piece to bond the cork to the top of the ceiling you just made.

Next, take another four piece cork and place it lying down and in the same direction as the other piece and place it on the left side of the piece you just glued. Using your glue gun, apply some glue on the left side of the piece and in between the two cork pieces.

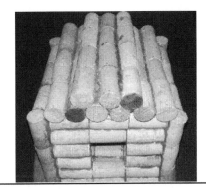

Now, take once more cork piece and lay it down the same way and up against the right side of the middle cork you applied a few moments ago. Apply some glue on the right side of the piece and in between the middle piece. You should now have 3 corks all lying down, facing the same direction, and all laid across the top of the ceiling of the birdhouse. The corks should all be facing the same direction as the ceiling corks. So, you should have 6 pieces of ceiling on top of the birdhouse then you should have 3 more pieces that are on top of but in between three of the corks that represent the ceiling.

You should have 1 more four piece cork left. Using your glue gun, apply some glue along the top of the middle cork piece of the 3 pieces you just installed. Apply the glue from one end of the piece to the other end. Place the last four cork piece, lying down, facing the same direction as the other pieces you just put in, and on top of the middle piece you just applied glue to. Allow a minute or two to dry and then apply glue any additional glue between the pieces on both sides. The top piece you just installed will be where the roof ends meet.

Before you install the roof, there are a few more pieces that are going to be needed. Lay the birdhouse aside and place a cork standing up on the table.

Apply some glue to the top of the cork and place another cork that is also standing up and on top of the cork you just applied the glue on. Again, apply some glue to the top of the cork and place a third cork standing up and on top of the other two corks. You should now have 3 corks all standing on top of each other and all pointing towards the ceiling.

Apply some glue to the top of the cork piece and again apply a fourth cork standing up and on top of the other three corks. Once more, apply some glue to the top of the four cork standing piece. Take one more cork, stand it up, and place it on top of the four corks that are standing.

 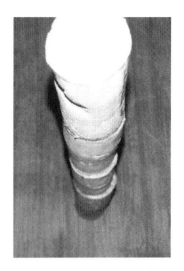

You should now have a total of 5 corks that are all standing up and all glued on top of each other. You only need one of these pieces. You are now ready to install the roof to the birdhouse.

Take the birdhouse and place it in on the table and with the front of the birdhouse facing you. Now using your glue gun, apply some glue along the top of the left cork piece of the ceiling. Apply the glue from one end of the piece to the other end of the piece. Next, apply some glue along the top of the left piece that is on top of the ceiling. Apply the glue from one end to the other end. Finally, apply glue along the top of the very top piece of the ceiling.

Apply glue to these three cork pieces as quickly as possible so that the glue doesn't dry up! Once the glue has been applied, take one side of the roof you made earlier and place it so that the cork ends are resting on the middle of the top cork piece. Place it on the very top four cork piece of the ceiling and not just up against it. Align the roof straight and so that the cork ends are resting against the middle of the top piece. Place the roof so that all the cork ends are pointing downward and at an angle.

Line up the roof so that it has one row of corks overhanging on both the front side and back side of the birdhouse. Try to have the roof also joining on the cork pieces you applied the glue. Allow a minute to dry and then apply glue in between the cork ends on top of the birdhouse so that the roof bonds to the birdhouse. Repeat the same process for the right side of the roof. Allow several minutes to dry before continuing.

Once the roof has dried, take the five cork piece you made a moment ago and lay it down so that the ends are pointing towards you and place it up against and in between the left side and right side on top of the roof. Apply some glue along the sides of the piece and secure the piece in place with the top of the roof. Make sure that all the ends are as even as possible with one another.

The only piece left to create is the front porch of the birdhouse. Take a cork and stand it up on the table.

  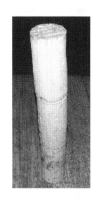

Place some glue to the top of the cork and place another cork standing up and on top of the cork you just apply glue. Once again, apply some glue to the top of the cork and place one more cork, standing up, on top of the two standing corks. You now have 3 corks all standing up and all attached to each other. Two of these pieces are needed, so create one more of these pieces consisting of 3 standing corks all standing and glued together. Once these two pieces are created, the front porch is ready to be made.

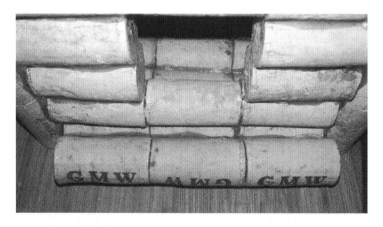

Place the birdhouse in front of you and with the front side facing you. Take one of the three cork pieces and lay it down sideways. Lay the piece up against the bottom cork row so that the corks are next to each other and the corks pointing the same direction as each other. Hold the piece in place and using your glue gun, apply some glue in between the two pieces so that they bond together.

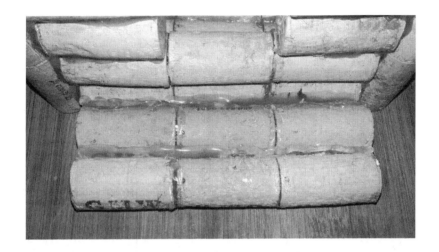

Allow a minute or two to dry and take the other three cork piece and lay it down sideways and up against the piece you just installed. Hold the piece up against the other piece and apply some glue in between the two pieces to bond the pieces together. Allow a couple minutes to dry and then carefully flip the birdhouse over and apply some glue in between the cork pieces to make them even stronger. Examine the birdhouse and apply additional glue anywhere needed around the birdhouse. Allow several minutes to dry and you have just created a really nice unique birdhouse!

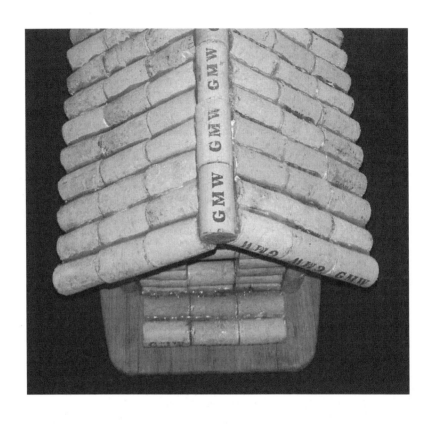

COOL UNIVERAL GOLF PUTTER

Create a golf putter that's universal and can be used whether you are left-handed or right-handed. This is a great novelty item and very simple to make. Start by laying a cork down on the table so that the ends of the cork are pointing sideways.

WHAT YOU NEED:

- Glue Gun
- Glue
- Marker or Pen
- Knife
- Cutting Board
- Gloves
- 22 Cork or Less

Estimated Time: 20 minutes

Next, place a cork standing up on top of and in the middle of the cork that is lying down on the table. Firmly hold the corks in place and with a pen or marker carefully draw the outline of the standing cork onto the cork that is lying down.

When you are done, there should be a circle drawn in the middle of the cork's body that is lying down on the table. Using a knife or hobby knife, carefully carve out the outline on the cork. It's a good idea to wear gloves when carving out the hole to protect your hands better. Carefully carve the outline of the circle about ¼ or close to ½ inch deep in the cork. Carve out the entire area inside the circle that you drew. Once the area has been carved out, take another cork and insert it into the hole.

If the cork will not fit, remove the cork and carefully take out the appropriate amount needed until the cork will securely fit standing up in the cork. Once the cork will fit securely in the cork, remove the cork and apply glue to the end of the cork that will be inserted in the cork. Also, apply glue to the hole that the cork will be inserted into. After the glue has been applied, insert the cork in the hole and make sure the cork is inserted straight and in a vertical position. Allow a minute to dry.

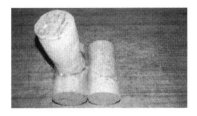 

Now, take a cork and lay it down the same way and with the cork end pointing towards you. Lay the cork against the body of the other cork that is lying down with the standing cork inserted in it. It should be lying down next to and against the body of the other cork that is lying down. Make sure the cork ends on both sides of the corks are even with each other. Firmly hold the corks in place and apply some glue in between the two corks from one end all the way to the other end so that they will securely bond together. Take another cork and lay it down against the cork you just attached. Lay the cork the same way the other two corks are laying and against the last cork you glued. Again, make sure the ends of all the corks are even with each other. Firmly hold the cork in place against the other two corks and apply glue in between the corks to bond the cork to the other two corks. You should now have three corks that are all lying down and bonded together. Once more, take another cork and lay it down against the cork you just attached. Lay the cork the same way the other three corks are laying and against the last cork you just glued. Again, make sure both ends of all the corks are even with each other. Firmly hold the cork in place against the last cork you glued and apply glue in between the corks to bond the cork to the other three corks. You should now have a total of four corks lying down beside each other and all bonded together.

On one side, you should have the cork with the vertical cork inserted in it. Next, take a cork and stand it up on the table. Apply some glue to the top of the cork and place another cork standing up on top of the cork you just applied the glue on. You should now have two corks standing up and one should be on the top of the other. Lay this piece aside and create one more just like this one.

Next take one of the 2 pieces you just made and lay it down sideways on the table. Lay the piece down against the front cork ends sideways so that the ends of the corks are touching the body of the cork you just laid down. Hold the pieces carefully in place and using your glue gun, apply some glue in between the corks to bond the front side piece.

Now take the remaining piece, lay it down on the table sideways and place it the same way and against the backside of the putter. Again place the body of the piece against the cork ends of the putter. Firmly hold the pieces in place and using your glue gun, apply some glue in between the two pieces so that they will bond together. This is your golf putter! Now it is time to create the handle to the putter. This will be easy.

Start by applying glue to the top of the vertical cork that is inserted in the putter. Take a cork and stand it up on top of the vertical piece you just applied the glue to.

Allow a few minutes to dry and then apply some glue to the top of the piece you just attached. Again, take another cork and stand it up on top of the cork you just applied the glue to. Repeat the process until you get the desired height of your handle. Keep in mind that every cork you add will add less stability and will cause the putter handle to become more flexible.

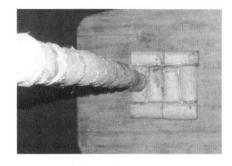

I used a total of 12 corks for the handle not counting the inserted cork. You can make the putter longer or shorter. Once your desired height has been reached, go back and apply any glue along the cork handle if there are any gaps or spaces between the cork pieces. Allow for few minutes for drying and then you will be ready to try out your custom putter. Add a couple plastic practice balls and take the putter to your office or to your living room! Make it a special gift for any golf enthusiasts! Creative gifts are the best gifts!

CRAFTY NAPKIN HOLDER

WHAT YOU NEED:

✕	Glue Gun
✎	Glue
✎	24 Cork

Estimated Time:

🕐 20 minutes

This crafty napkin holder will be useful for the years to come! It's easy to make and doesn't take long to construct.

Start by taking a cork and laying it down on the table so that the end of the cork is pointing toward you. Take another cork and lay it down the exact same way and directly beside the cork that is already lying down. Press the corks together and make sure both cork ends are flush and even with each other. Hold the corks firmly together and with your glue gun, apply glue in between the two corks from one end to the other end.

Keep holding the corks together for about a minute to allow the glue to dry and then flip over the piece. Apply glue in between the corks from one end to the other. This will represent one piece and you are going to need 12 pieces total. Since you just created one piece, you still need to create 11 more of these pieces. Once all 12 pieces have been created, you are ready to move on and begin construction.

Next, take one of the 12 cork pieces you just created and stand the piece up on the table. Using your glue gun, apply some glue along the top of both corks. Now, take another cork piece and place it standing up and on top of the piece you just applied the glue to. Make sure that both cork pieces are lined up with each other.

Allow a minute for the piece to dry then lay the piece down on the table. Apply glue in between the corks, wait a minute or so and then flip it over to the other side. Again, apply glue in between the corks to help strengthen the corks. This will be the bottom of the napkin holder. Now, lay the bottom of the napkin holder aside.

Now you are ready to use the remaining pieces you created earlier for the front and back of the napkin holder. Take one of the two cork pieces and lay it down on the table so that the cork ends are pointing towards you.

Next, take another one of the two cork pieces and place the piece up against the body and beside the piece that is already lying down. Both pieces should be against the other and they are touching the body of each other. Both pieces should be pointing towards you. Be sure the pieces are lined up good with each other and that the ends are both even with each other.

Hold the two pieces firmly together in place and using your glue gun, apply glue in between the two pieces to bond the pieces together. Allow a minute or so to dry. Flip the piece over and apply glue in between the two pieces to strengthen the piece even more. This piece will be part of the front or part of the back of the napkin holder. You will need to create 4 more of these pieces. So, using the 8 remaining two-cork pieces you made earlier create 4 more pieces like the one you just made. Each piece has 2 two cork pieces bonded together making four corks total.

Once all 5 pieces have been made, you can move on with the project!

Take one of the four cork pieces you just finished making and stand it up on the table with the cork ends pointing towards the ceiling.

Using your glue gun, apply some glue along the top of the corks. Now take another four cork piece you just made and place it standing up and on top of the corks you just applied the glue on.

You should have four corks standing on top of four corks that are also standing. This piece is a total of eight corks and will be the front of the napkin holder. The back of the napkin holder is similar but will require one more layer of corks making a total of twelve corks.

Using the remaining 3 four cork pieces, stand one of the pieces up on the table and with your glue gun, apply some glue along the top of the corks. Take another four cork piece, stand it up, and place the piece on top of the four corks you just applied the glue on. Even the corks up with each other the best you can. Once more, using your glue gun, apply some glue along the top of the corks. Finally, take the last four cork piece and place it standing up on top of the corks you just applied to the glue to.

You should now have a total of 12 corks all glued together and all standing up pointing towards the ceiling. This piece is the back of the napkin holder.

Now that you have the front and back of the napkin holder, all the pieces have been created and now you are ready to put the crafty napkin holder together! Start by taking the bottom of the napkin holder you created earlier and laying it down on the table sideways, so that the cork ends are pointing from left to right.

Now take the back of the napkin holder or the 12 cork piece. Stand the piece up and with the cork ends pointing towards the ceiling. Place the piece on the backside and against the bottom piece. Place it so that the piece is against the body of the bottom piece and not on top of the bottom piece.

Be sure to even the ends of both pieces with each other as best as possible. Carefully hold the pieces together and using your glue gun, apply glue to the inside of where the two pieces meet to bond the pieces together. Allow a minute or so to dry and then go back over and add any extra glue needed to fill in the gaps between the pieces. Allow a minute or so to dry then take the remaining eight cork piece and stand it up and against the front of the bottom piece.

Again the corks are pointing the same direction from left to right. Firmly holding the pieces against one another take your glue gun and apply glue in between the two pieces to bond these pieces together. Again, allow a minute to dry and then go back over and apply any necessary glue needed to fill in the gaps between the pieces. Allow a minute or so to dry and then carefully flip over the piece. Using your glue gun, apply glue in between the pieces on the bottom and the sides to add more durability for the holder. Allow a minute to dry and flip the napkin holder back over to its original position.

If any additional glue is needed, apply glue inside the napkin holder to fill in the small holes or gaps that are between the front and back pieces connected to the bottom of the holder. Allow a few minutes for the glue to dry. You are ready to add your napkins and start using your new authentic and crafty napkin holder!

USEFUL CELL PHONE OR TABLET STAND

A handmade cell phone or tablet stand that is handy to use at your office or anywhere in your house! This stand keeps your tablet or phone more visible and more protected than just laying it on the table or your desk at the office. It's easy to make and doesn't require many corks! Start by taking a cork and laying it down on the table so that the end of the cork is pointing toward you.

WHAT YOU NEED:
- Glue Gun
- Glue
- 20 Corks

Estimated Time:
- 20 minutes

Take another cork and lay it down the same way and directly up against the body of the cork that is already lying down, so that the body of each cork is touching each other. Press the corks together and make sure both cork ends are even with each other. Hold the corks firmly together and with your glue gun, apply glue in between the two corks from one end of the corks to the other end. Keep holding the corks together for about a minute to allow the glue to dry and then carefully flip over the piece. Apply glue in between the corks again from one end of the corks to the other end.

Take another cork, lay it down the same way and again repeat this process until you have a total of 6 corks all glued to the body of each other and attached together. All 6 corks are laying down, all pointing in the same direction, even on the ends with one another, and all glued to each another. Lay this piece aside and create one more piece just like this one. Return to the top of this paragraph and repeat this step.

You should now have two separate cork pieces but each piece has 6 corks attached to it. Once these two pieces have been created, you are ready to continue with the project.

Next, take one of the 6 cork pieces and stand the piece up on the table so that the ends of the corks are pointing upwards toward the ceiling. Apply glue to the top of all 6 corks. Take your other 6 cork piece and stand the piece up the exact same way and on top of the piece you just applied the glue to. Try to align the corks even with each other the best way possible. Allow a minute to dry and then lay the piece down on the table. Apply some additional glue along the middle of the piece or where the corks meet up. This will add more durability and strength. Once you have applied glue along where all the cork ends meet, allow a minute to dry and then flip the piece over. Again, apply some glue to the middle of the piece and where the corks meet up with one another. This piece is the back of the cell phone or tablet stand. Lay this piece aside and allow it to dry. It will be used soon but first you need to create a couple more pieces.

Now, take a cork and lay it down on the table so that the end of the cork is pointing toward you. Take another cork and lay it down the same way and directly against the body of the cork that is already lying down. Lay it down so that the body of both corks is touching each other. Make sure the corks ends are even with each other. Press and hold the corks firmly together.

Using your glue gun, apply glue in between both corks from one end to the other end. Keep the corks held together for about a minute to allow the pieces to bond together and then carefully flip the piece over. Apply glue in between the corks from one end to the other end. This will be one piece and you will need 4 pieces total. The remaining corks that are needed in this project are used to create these pieces. You should have 6 corks remaining which will make 3 more of these pieces.

Next, take one of the pieces you just created and stand it up on the table. Using your glue gun, apply some glue to the top of both corks. Take one of the remaining cork pieces and place it on top of the piece you applied the glue. Stand the cork piece up and on top of the other piece, try to even up the corks together, and hold both cork pieces firmly in place. Place this piece aside and create one more piece just like this one. Using the last 2 cork pieces remaining, stand one of the pieces up on the table. With your glue gun, apply some glue to the top of both cork pieces. Place the remaining cork piece standing up and on top of the piece you just applied the glue to. Again, try to even the corks together and hold the cork pieces firmly in place for a minute so that it will bond good.

This should leave you with a total of 3 separate cork pieces. Two pieces should be the same and consist of 4 corks each and the third piece should consist of 12 corks. This will be the front, bottom, and back of the cell phone stand. It's now time to assemble the pieces together.

Start by taking your 12 cork piece and stand it up on the table so that the cork ends are all pointing sideways from left to right. You will have to hold this piece in its upright position. Take one of the four cork pieces and lay it down on the table. Position the corks the exact same way and against the front body of the piece you are holding that is standing up. You may have to reposition your hands but you need to bond these two pieces together. Take your glue gun and apply glue in between the two pieces to attach the pieces together. Firmly hold the piece in place for a minute to make sure the pieces are bonded together. Make sure the ends are even with one another and make sure the standing piece is as vertically straight as possible and then carefully flip the piece over and again apply some glue in between the cork pieces to help strengthen the corks together. Once the pieces are securely attached to one another, carefully flip the piece back over and stand it up. This is the way you had it positioned a moment ago when you attached the two pieces to each other. Now you are ready to attach the final piece.

Finally, take the remaining 4 cork piece and stand it up but so that the cork ends are also pointing sideways. You will have to hold this piece up. Place the piece against the front body of corks so that both cork pieces are touching together and the corks are pointing sideways. Hold the pieces firmly in place. You may have to reposition your hands here but take your glue gun and apply glue in between the two cork pieces to attach them together. Allow a minute or so to dry while holding the piece in place. Then flip the piece over. Again, apply glue using your glue gun in between the cork pieces to help bond them more securely and make the cell phone stand stronger. Also, examine the entire piece over and add any necessary glue in between any corks that looks like they may need it. Allow a couple minutes for the entire piece to dry and then add your phone or tablet to your new stand!

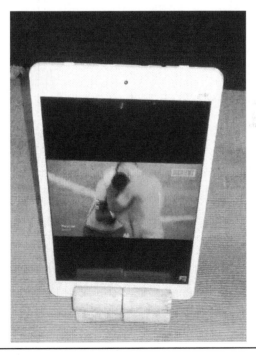

ELEGANT BUSINESS CARD HOLDER

This business card holder adds a cozy elegant look and touch to your office or home office.

WHAT YOU NEED:	
✖	Glue Gun
✏	Glue
✏	12 Corks
Estimated Time:	
⏱	10 minutes

Start by taking a cork and standing it up on the table so that the end of the cork is pointing towards the ceiling. Using your glue gun, apply some glue to the top of the cork.

Now, take another cork and stand it up and place it on top of the cork you just applied the glue to. You should now have two corks glued together. Both corks are pointing upwards and one cork is on top of the other cork. You will need 6 of these pieces total. You just created one, so create 5 more pieces like the one you just made. Once all 6 pieces have been created, you are ready to move on with the project.

Take one of the 6 pieces you just created and lay it down on the table with the cork end pointing towards you. Now take another one of the pieces and lay it down on the table the exact same way and against the body of the cork already lying on the table. Even the ends up with each other and firmly hold the pieces together. Using your glue gun, apply glue in between the corks from one end to the other to bond the two pieces together. You should have two cork pieces glued together and lying down on the table. Flip this piece over and apply glue in between the corks from one end to the other. You need 3 of these pieces to complete this project. Create 2 more of these pieces the exact same way before moving on with the project.

After all 3 pieces have been made the business card holder is ready to be assembled. Now take one of the 3

pieces and lay it down on the table so that the ends are pointing sideways from left to right. Using your glue gun, apply glue along the top of the back cork piece from one end to the other end. The back cork piece is the piece farthest away from you. Take another one of the pieces and stand it up sideways so that the corks from both pieces line up with each other. Stand this piece up with the corks pointing sideways and on top of the piece you just applied the glue on. Carefully hold the two pieces in place and keep the piece that is standing up as vertical as possible. Allow a few minutes to dry and then take the piece and apply any extra glue needed on both sides where the two pieces meet.

Once any extra glue has been added, place it back on the table the exact way you had it a moment ago, with the ends of the corks pointing from left to right. Now take the last piece you have and place it standing up but sideways and with the cork ends pointing left to right. Place this piece in front of and against the business card holder. Keep the piece as vertical as possible and make sure the cork ends are even with each other. Carefully hold the two pieces in place. Using your glue gun, apply glue in between the two pieces to attach the front side with the rest of the business card holder. This will most likely be a little more difficult because of the spacing in between the back and the front of the business card holder. I found it easier to keep the pieces against one another but to slightly angle the front piece you are attaching. After angling the front piece, apply glue in between the cork pieces from one end of the piece all the way to the other end.

Then position the front piece back to its upright position so that it is vertical and straight. Allow a few minutes for the piece to dry. Now flip over the piece and apply any additional glue in between the two pieces to make the card holder stronger. Again, allow a few minutes to dry then add your business cards and put your elegant business card holder to good use!

Additional Cork Crafting Ideas

Nautical Cork Keychain

Pen/Pencil Holder

Necklace

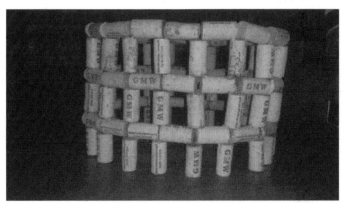

Replica of Rome's Coliseum

Thank you for taking the time and choosing Wine Cork Crafting! I hope you found the projects fun and exciting to make. Your possibilities with corks are endless!

INDEX

What are corks?	i
Easy Refrigerator Magnets	7
Cool Picture Frame	10
Nifty Table Trivet	19
Distinctive Wine Rack	24
Effective Drink Coasters	36
Single Wine Bottle Holder	40
Aquarium Sailboat	53
Detailed Model Airplane	56
Super Simple Model Car	62
Floating Castaway Sailboat	66
Fancy European Car Model	70
Civil War Cannon	76
Creative Birdhouse	82
Cool Universal Golf Putter	113
Crafty Napkin Holder	120
Useful Cell Phone or Tablet Stand	128
Elegant Business Card Holder	136
Additional Cork Crafting Ideas	140

Made in the USA
Columbia, SC
14 November 2022